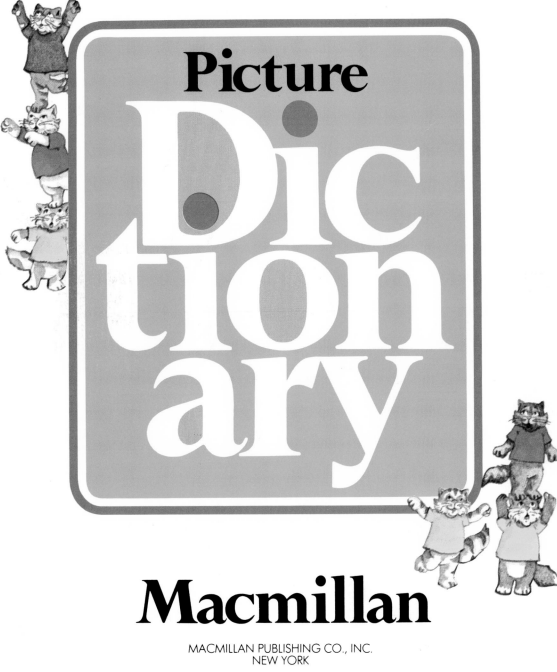

Picture Dictionary

Macmillan

MACMILLAN PUBLISHING CO., INC.
NEW YORK

COLLIER MACMILLAN PUBLISHERS
LONDON

Macmillan Publishing Co., Inc.
866 Third Avenue, New York, N.Y. 10022
Collier Macmillan Canada, Inc.

Printed in the United States of America
This dictionary is also published in a trade edition
under the title *The Macmillan Picture Wordbook*.

10 9 8 7 6 5 4 3 2

ISBN 0-02-195120-9

CONTENTS

HOW TO HELP YOUR STUDENTS

The Macmillan Picture Dictionary is designed to do more than just teach words. As young readers-to-be match pictures with words, they take a first giant step towards learning to read. Leafing through the book provides a combination of fun and achievement. Each page offers entertainment, discovery, and identification. In addition, there are games that can be played with the words and pictures throughout the book. Here are some suggestions:

1 **Find the Cat.** On almost every page of this book, there is a little cat somewhere in the picture. Sometimes it is nearly hidden, other times it is easy to see, but always it relates to the family of words being introduced.

2 **I Spy.** As you enjoy the book with your students, take turns saying, "I spy something red," or, "I spy something round," or, "I spy something with four legs." When the students find the matching picture, point to the word, say it, and ask them to repeat it. Then change about and let a student be the "spy."

3 **A Child's Own Word List.** Play "I Spy" with objects in sight of you and your students. Ask them to try and find pictures of the objects in the Dictionary. If an object is not in this Dictionary, start a personal word list by writing the word down and then searching for a picture of the word in magazines and catalogs. They provide great illustrations for a child's very own book, and it is fun to cut and paste.

USE THIS BOOK

4 **I Remember.** Ask your students to remember people, animals, places, and activities that they have recently seen. See if the students can find them in the Dictionary. If not, make another entry in the child's own word list. Learning the words to describe a personal experience is exciting and will lead to rewarding language skills.

5 **Grandma's Trunk.** A very unusual grandma is packing her trunk with anything that begins with, say, the letter B. Look through the book and see what begins with B: bear, butter, bed, beads….Nothing is out of bounds for this funny grandma. A variation of this game could have grandma choose one object from each letter of the alphabet.

6 **Learning To Use a Dictionary.** A dictionary is a wordbook in ABC (alphabetical) order. It also explains what a word means. If a student doesn't understand a word, or if he or she would like to know more about it, look it up in a dictionary. Here is a good way to introduce the use of a dictionary: Turn to any page in this book, look at the words, and, with the help of the child, list them in alphabetical order. It is useful to have a separate card for each letter of the alphabet: an A card, a B card, and so on. The alphabet pages of this book (Apple-Pie ABC on pages 78 and 79) will show the child the order of the letters.

Above all, have fun with this book. Let your students go at their own pace, either lingering over a page or skimming on to the next one. Gradually, with growing interest and a feeling of success, the children will grasp the connection between the picture and the printed word that goes with it. Now turn the pages and enjoy the thrill of helping the reader-to-be discover a love and appreciation of words that will always be treasured.

Houses

adobe house

Houses are where people live. There are hundreds of different kinds of houses, in towns and cities and in the country, in hot countries and cold countries. What kind of house do you live in?

mobile home

grass hut

Japanese paper house

desert tent

tepee

igloo

underground house

solar house

roof

skylight

antenna

attic

bathroom

window shutters

window box

stairs

bedroom

garage

kitchen

dining room

living room

front door

driveway

bushes

steps

dryer

washing machine

tools

workbench

hot-water tank

grass

furnace

basement

7

BREAKFAST

orange juice

toaster

cup

coffee pot

orange

squeezer

saucer

cream pitcher

cereal

milk

jam

spoon

cat's dish

bowl

egg

knife

bacon

toast

butter

sugar bowl

Mealtimes

You eat breakfast in the morning. Lunch is a meal that you have at noon. In the evening you usually eat the biggest meal of the day, which is dinner. Sometimes it is called supper. Maybe you have a favorite snack in between meals.

LUNCH

thermos

peanut butter and jelly sandwich

lunch box

napkin

cookies

milk

carrot sticks

straw

paper plate

fork

cottage cheese

school books

8

DINNER

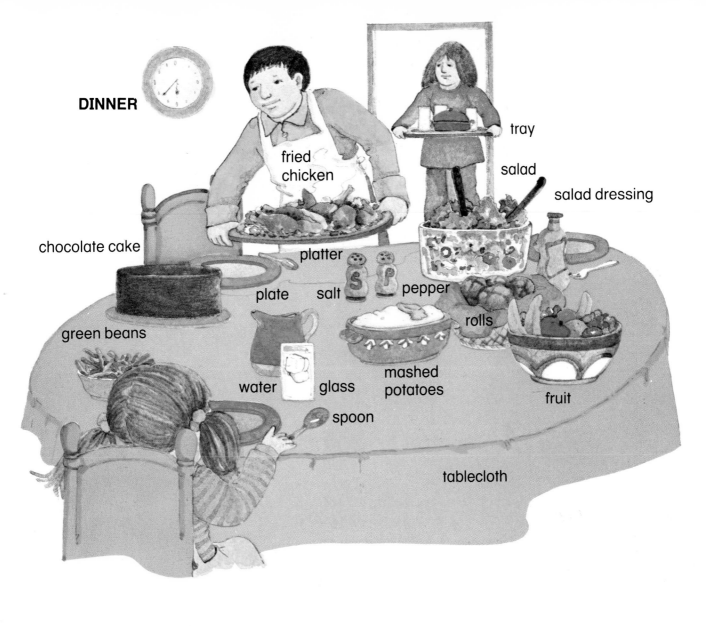

fried chicken

tray

salad

salad dressing

chocolate cake

platter

plate salt pepper

rolls

green beans

water glass

mashed potatoes

fruit

spoon

tablecloth

SNACK TIME

storybook

popcorn

oatmeal cookies

grapes

Bill's Best

cheese

milk

celery sticks

cat snack

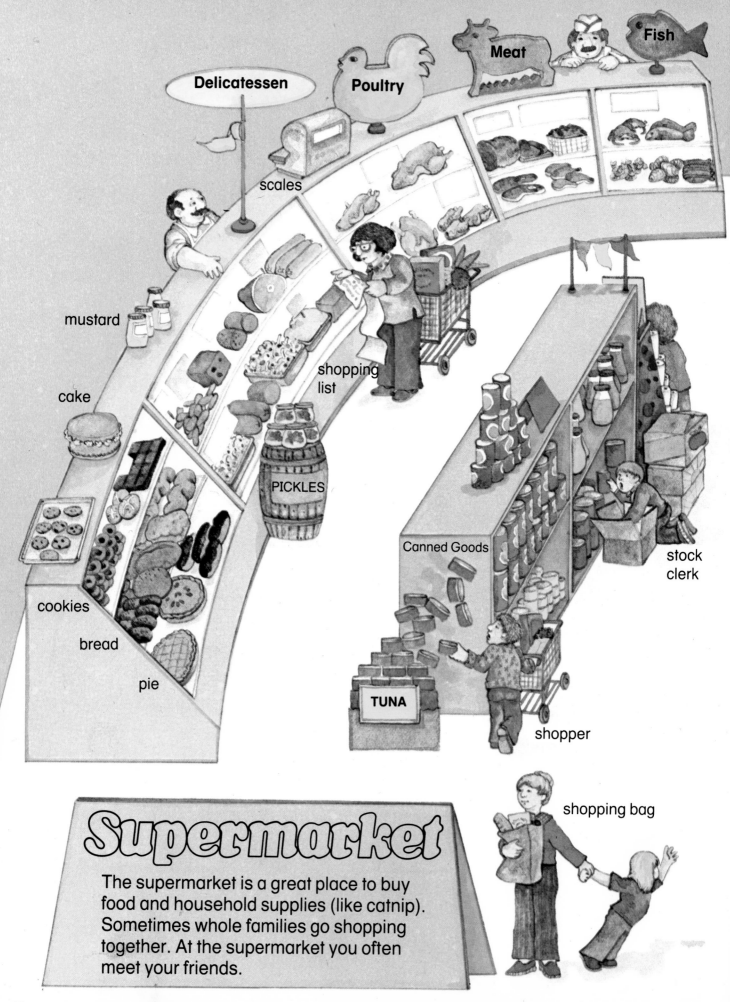

Delicatessen

Poultry

Meat

Fish

scales

mustard

shopping list

cake

PICKLES

cookies

bread

pie

Canned Goods

stock clerk

TUNA

shopper

shopping bag

Supermarket

The supermarket is a great place to buy food and household supplies (like catnip). Sometimes whole families go shopping together. At the supermarket you often meet your friends.

Fruits and Vegetables

scales

soft drinks   ice cream

frozen foods

household supplies

milk

TV dinner

pizza

cat food

cottage cheese

eggs

flour

cereal

yogurt

PEANUT BUTTER

butter

margarine

cheese

sugar

checkout counter

cash register

money

checker

clerk

cart

Dairy

11

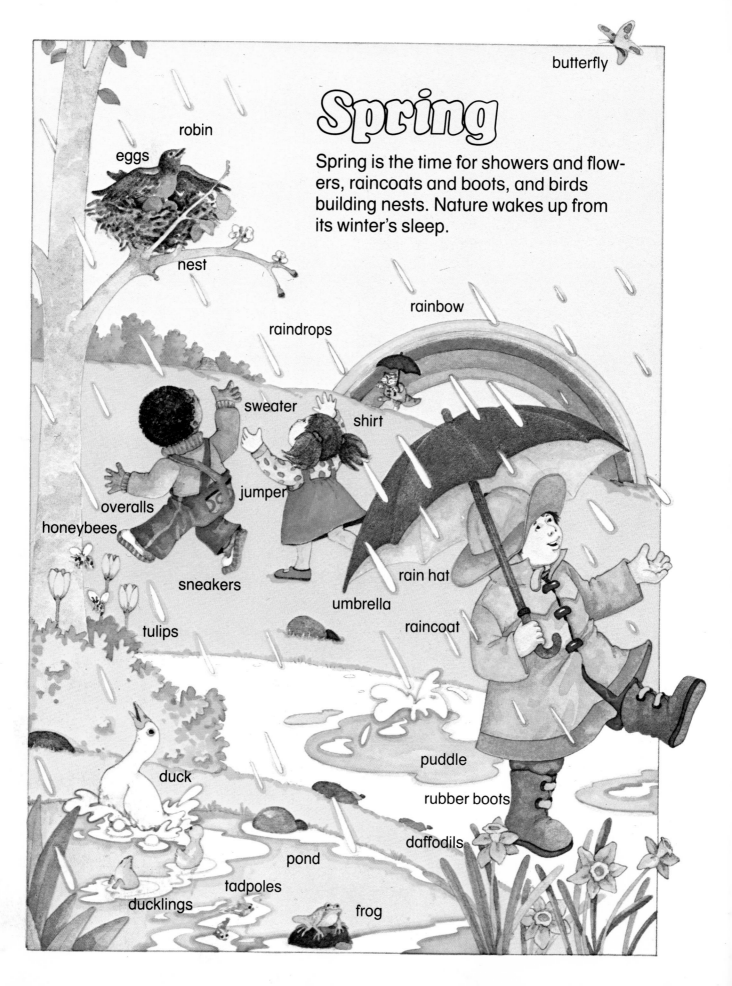

butterfly

robin

eggs

nest

Spring

Spring is the time for showers and flowers, raincoats and boots, and birds building nests. Nature wakes up from its winter's sleep.

rainbow

raindrops

sweater

shirt

jumper

overalls

honeybees

rain hat

sneakers

umbrella

raincoat

tulips

puddle

duck

rubber boots

daffodils

pond

tadpoles

ducklings

frog

Summer

Summer is the warmest time of the year. Many people go on vacation in the summer. They may go to the country or to the seashore. They may have picnics in the park. Ants have a wonderful time at picnics.

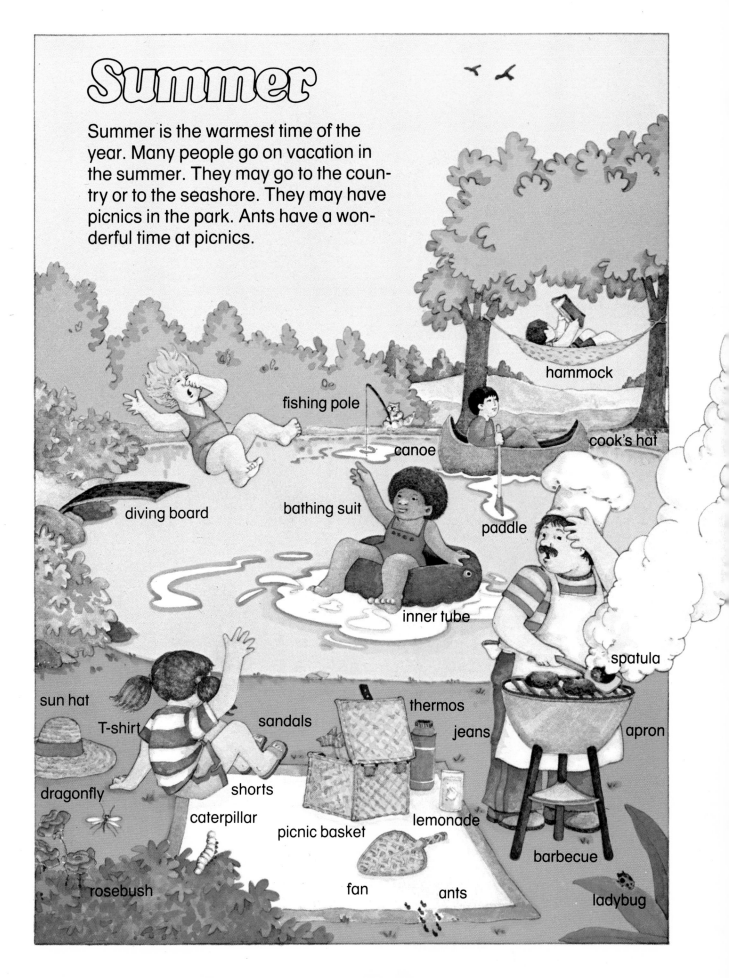

hammock

fishing pole

canoe

cook's hat

diving board

bathing suit

paddle

inner tube

spatula

sun hat

T-shirt

sandals

thermos

jeans

apron

dragonfly

shorts

caterpillar

picnic basket

lemonade

barbecue

rosebush

fan

ants

ladybug

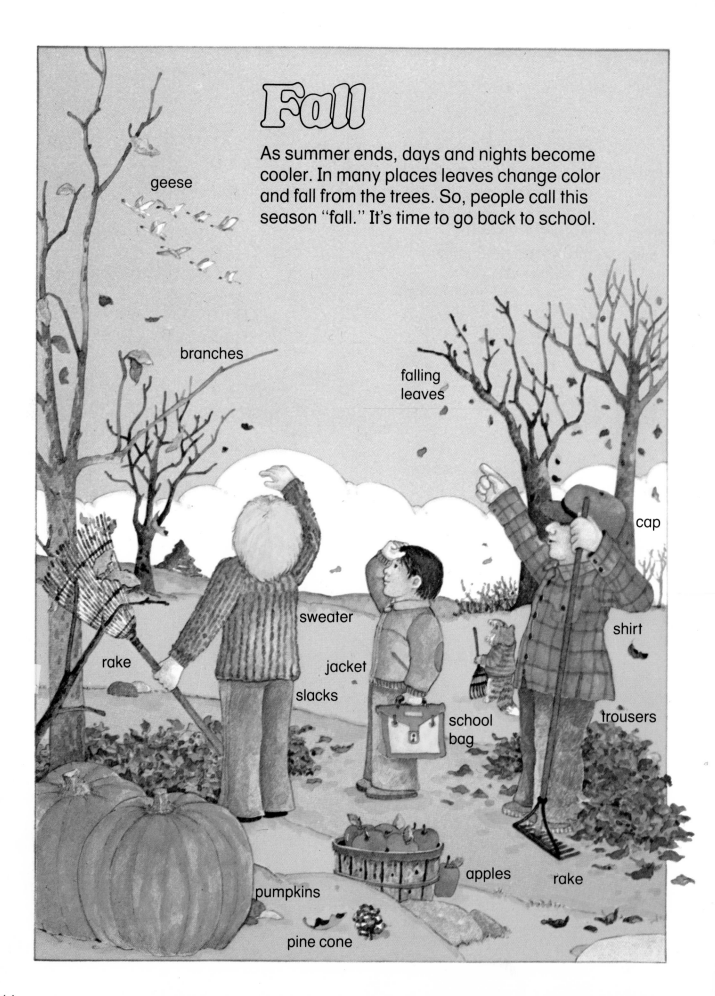

Fall

As summer ends, days and nights become cooler. In many places leaves change color and fall from the trees. So, people call this season "fall." It's time to go back to school.

geese

branches

falling leaves

cap

sweater

shirt

jacket

slacks

rake

school bag

trousers

apples

rake

pumpkins

pine cone

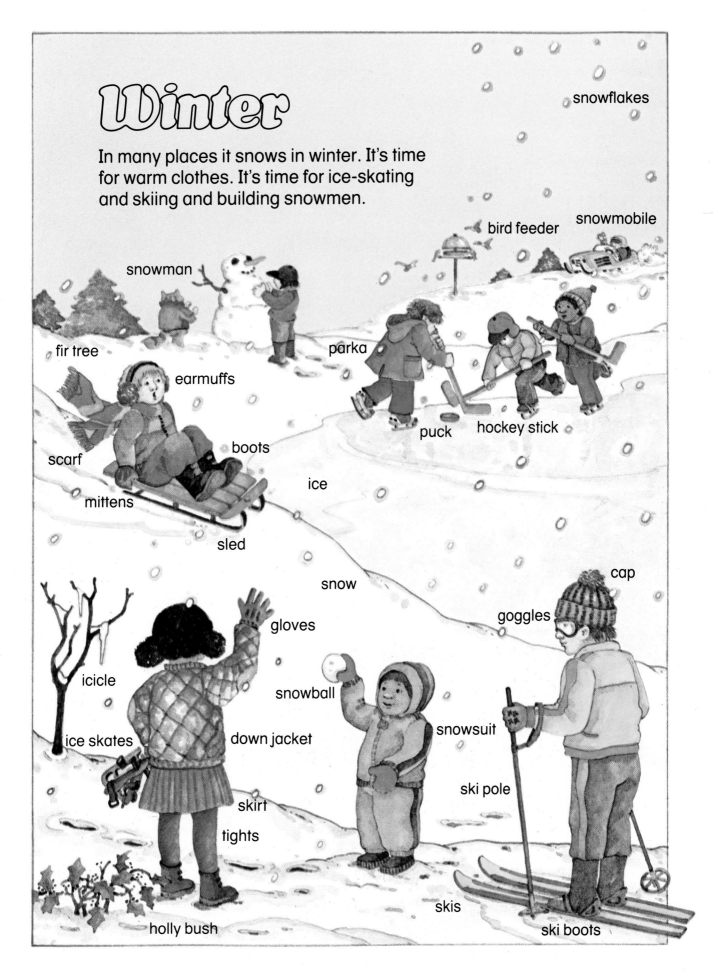

Winter

In many places it snows in winter. It's time for warm clothes. It's time for ice-skating and skiing and building snowmen.

snowflakes

bird feeder

snowmobile

snowman

fir tree

parka

earmuffs

scarf

boots

puck

hockey stick

mittens

ice

sled

snow

cap

gloves

goggles

icicle

snowball

snowsuit

ice skates

down jacket

ski pole

skirt

tights

skis

holly bush

ski boots

money

guards

armored car

jeep

car

sports car

Wheels on the Road

Big wheels, little wheels, cycle wheels, truck wheels — almost everything that moves has wheels. See how many more wheels you can find in other pictures.

crash helmet

goggles

moped

tow truck

wrecked car

repairman

bus

double-decker bus

lights

passengers

bus driver

police officer

flat tire

crash helmet

motorcycle

police car

16

Caterpillar tractor

earthmover

bulldozer

ditchdigger

road grader

dump truck

concrete spreader

surveyor

strike-off board

cement mixer

More Wheels

Before wheels can get rolling, people and machines must build roads and highways. It takes many busy people to keep roads in good shape. Look for more wheels in this book. There are lots.

guard rail

FRESH *Daisy Dairy* MILK

tank trailer

highway light

Soft Shoulder

cherry picker

road

road cap

car transporter

Ace Gravel Co.

dump truck

road barrier

repair truck

road roller

The City

A city is an exciting place. Here, thousands of people live and work day and night. Other people visit a city to see the big buildings, to enjoy themselves, and to do business. Many stop to watch a sky-scraper being built.

police officer

office building

bus

police officer

Cafe

STORE

DRESSES

Newsstand

BUS STOP

CINEMA

TICKETS

ANTIQUES

parking meter

fire hydrant

MEN WORKING

manhole cover

manhole

subway train

hot-dog cart

MAIL

mailbox

21

spire

rose window

cathedral

temple

Alex's

restaurant

steeple

bell tower

church

stained-glass window

museum

TOYS

store

22

minaret

dome

balcony

apartment building

mosque

synagogue

stadium

skyscraper

library

POST OFFICE

post office

LIBRARY

Buildings

Your house is a building that is special to you.
There are other special buildings. They are
places where people work, read, learn, play,
eat, and worship. Look for more buildings in
this book.

tree surgeon

fisherman

librarian

factory workers

artist

doorman

hairdresser

guard

mail carrier

bank teller

painter

24

waiter

chef

scientist

cameraman

judge

lawyer

mechanic

newscaster

People at Work

Here are some people working at their occupations. There are many other jobs that people do. You can find some of them in this book. What do you dream of doing when you grow up?

computer operator

plumber

salesperson

miner

factory

container

warehouse

container ship

tugboat

motorboat

tugboat

crane

pulleys

sailor

cargo

life preserver

hold

bow (front)

S.S. SEACAT

anchor

dock

harbor master

cargo

26

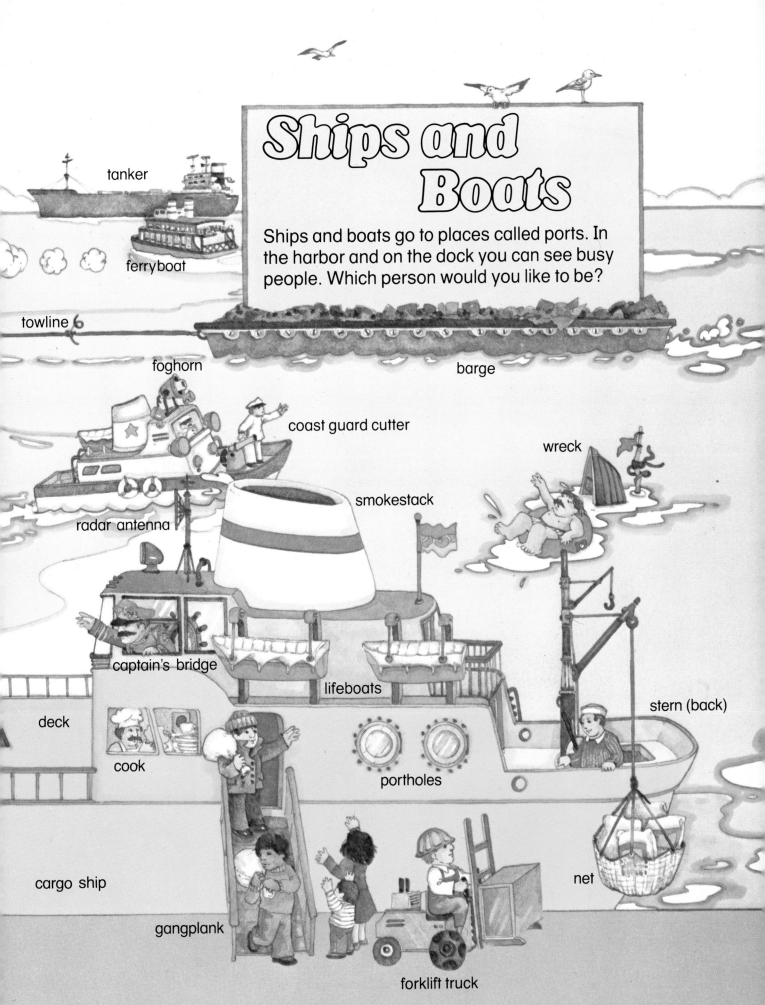

Ships and Boats

Ships and boats go to places called ports. In the harbor and on the dock you can see busy people. Which person would you like to be?

tanker

ferryboat

towline

foghorn

barge

coast guard cutter

wreck

smokestack

radar antenna

captain's bridge

lifeboats

deck

cook

portholes

stern (back)

cargo ship

net

gangplank

forklift truck

wind speed gauge

parachute

windsock

radar scanner

restaurant

runway lights

control tower

observation deck

parking lot

CAR RENTAL

The Airport

An airport is a place where all kinds of airplanes take off and land on the runways. Some carry cargo. Many of them carry hundreds of passengers. Small airplanes may hold only two people. Have you ever gone to an airport?

FOOD

EXIT ENTRANCE

SHOPS

CHECK-IN

ARRIVAL

DEPARTURE

tickets

LUGGAGE

porter

baggage cart

INFORMATION

automatic doors

tail

runway

pilot

wing   fuselage

cabin

flight attendant

mechanic

baggage
compartment

cargo loader

landing
gear

jet engine

passengers

FUEL

baggage truck

public address system

newsstand   restrooms   telephones   gates

MEN   WOMEN

water
fountain

GATE 16   GATE 17

security check

waiting room

Trains

Long before there were airplanes or buses, trains carried people and freight along hundreds of miles of railroad tracks across the country. The locomotive pulled the train of cars through tunnels in the mountains and across bridges over the rivers.

caboose

tunnel

crossing signal

crossing gate

railroad crossing

signal tower

switch box

diesel locomotive

conductor

flatcar

timber

coupling

tank car

boxcar

girder

trestle bridge

smoke

station

GREYWOOD

Waiting Room

Tickets

station master

platform

engineer

fender

steam locomotive

passengers

ties

railroad tracks

passenger car

31

School

You go to school to learn all kinds of things: reading, writing, spelling, drawing, music. You learn how to take care of animals. And you learn to play games and make friends with other children.

piano

goldfish

songbook

guitar

baton

record player

Music Corner

record albums

Quiet Corner

hand bells

tambourine

pillow

teacher

drum

blanket

drumsticks

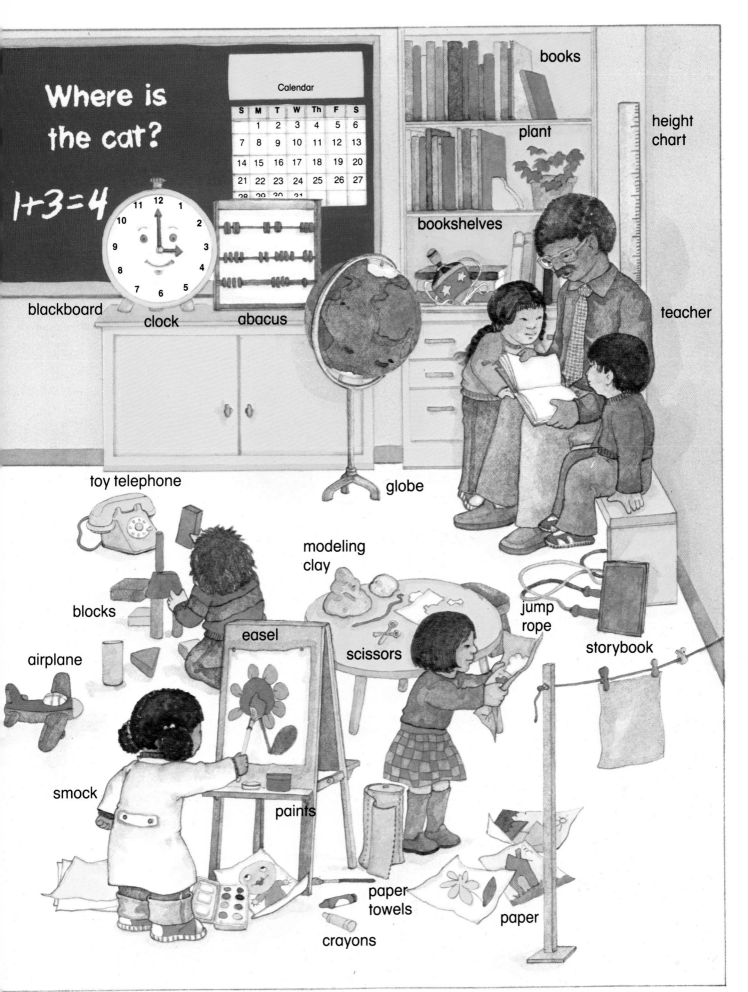

Where is the cat?

1+3=4

blackboard

clock

abacus

Calendar

S	M	T	W	Th	F	S
			1	2	3	4	5	6
7	8	9	10	11	12	13
14	15	16	17	18	19	20
21	22	23	24	25	26	27
28	29	30	31			

books

plant

height chart

bookshelves

teacher

toy telephone

globe

modeling clay

blocks

jump rope

storybook

easel

scissors

airplane

smock

paints

paper towels

paper

crayons

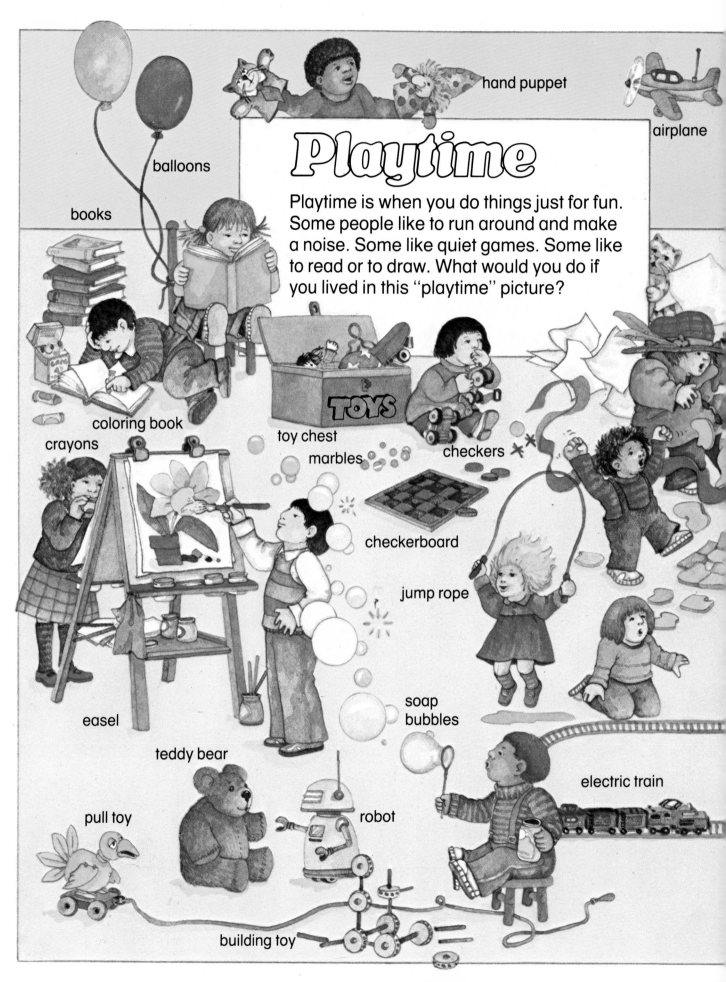

hand puppet

airplane

Playtime

Playtime is when you do things just for fun. Some people like to run around and make a noise. Some like quiet games. Some like to read or to draw. What would you do if you lived in this "playtime" picture?

balloons

books

coloring book

crayons

toy chest

marbles

checkers

checkerboard

jump rope

easel

teddy bear

soap bubbles

pull toy

robot

electric train

building toy

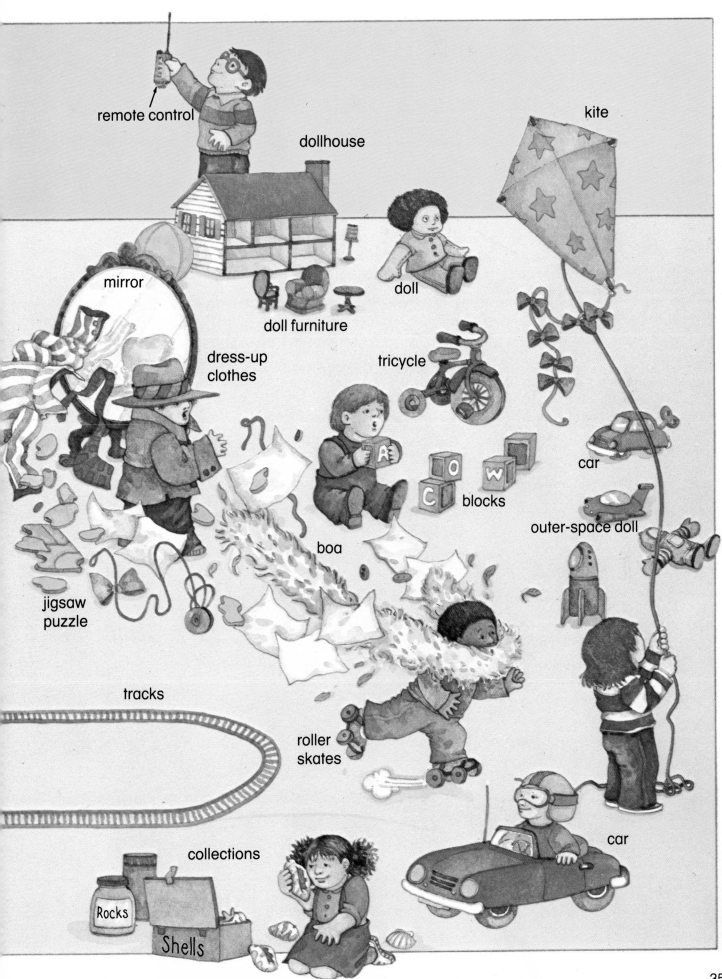

remote control

kite

dollhouse

doll

mirror

doll furniture

dress-up
clothes

tricycle

car

blocks

outer-space doll

boa

jigsaw
puzzle

tracks

roller
skates

collections

car

Rocks

Shells

Sports

Sports are games that we play. People everywhere enjoy playing and watching sports. They can go to see them "live," or they can watch them on television.

stadium

helmet

shoulder pad

face guard

football

referee

cheer leaders

players

goal post

knee pad

FOOTBALL

thigh pad

hip pad

cleated shoes

backboard

scoreboard

hoop

basketball

net

BASKETBALL

coach

referee

1st base

36

umpire

racket

TENNIS

ball

net

lines

tennis court

soccer ball

net

SOCCER

goal

players

field

stadium

umpire

bat

batter

ball

mitt

cap

mask

chest
protector

catcher

shin
guards

home
plate

3rd base

pitcher

2nd base

BASEBALL

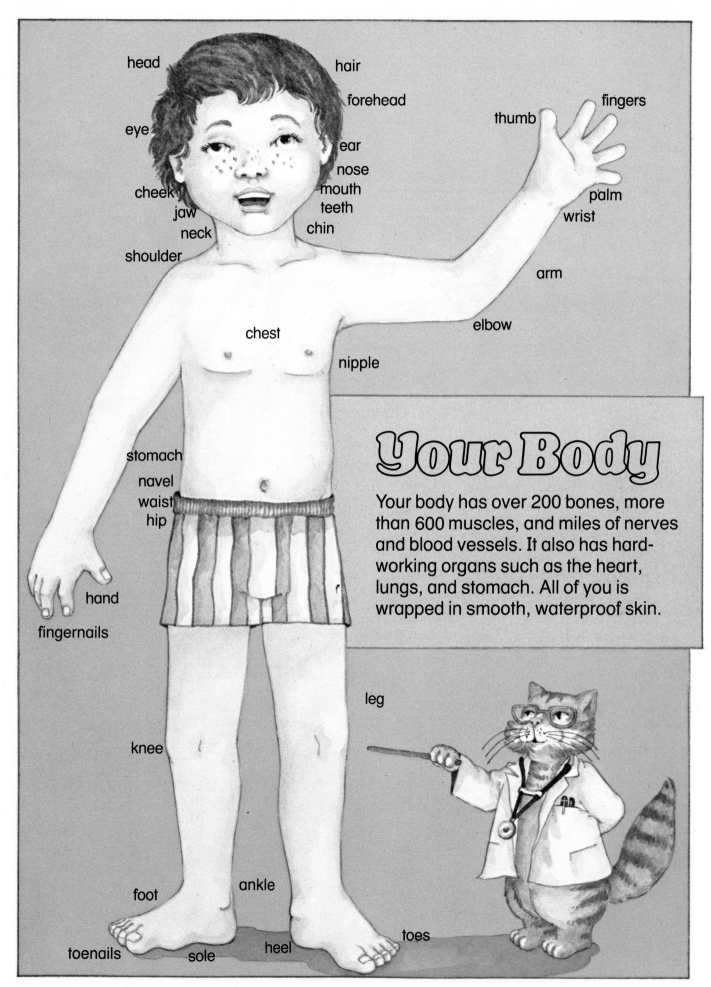

head

hair

forehead

fingers

thumb

eye

ear

nose

mouth

teeth

chin

palm

wrist

cheek

jaw

neck

arm

shoulder

elbow

chest

nipple

Your Body

Your body has over 200 bones, more than 600 muscles, and miles of nerves and blood vessels. It also has hard-working organs such as the heart, lungs, and stomach. All of you is wrapped in smooth, waterproof skin.

stomach

navel

waist

hip

hand

fingernails

leg

knee

foot

ankle

toes

toenails

sole

heel

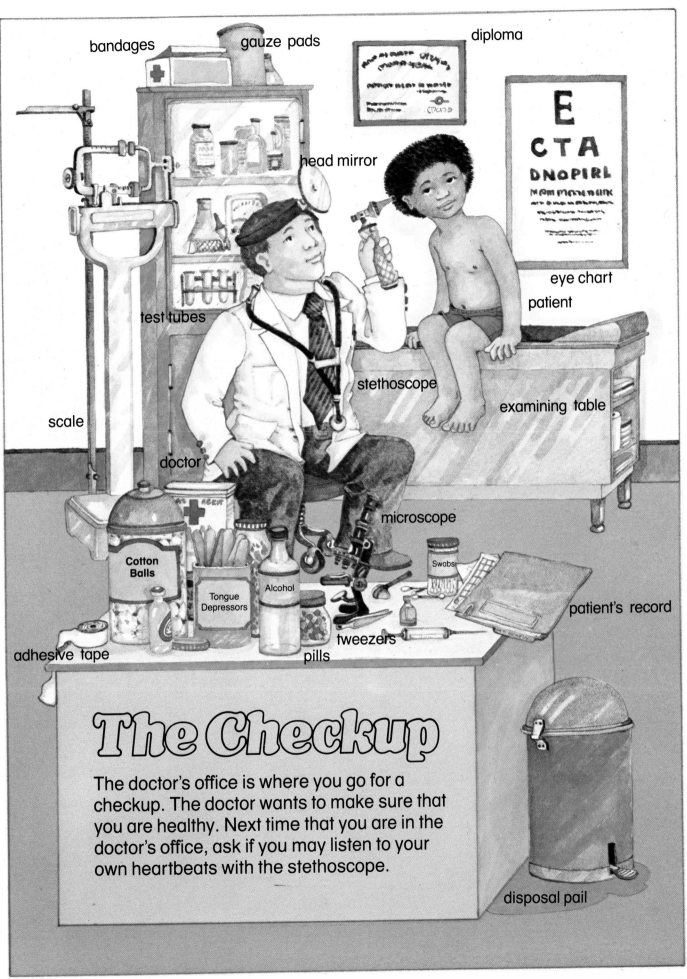

bandages

gauze pads

diploma

head mirror

test tubes

stethoscope

eye chart

patient

examining table

scale

doctor

microscope

Cotton Balls

Tongue Depressors

Alcohol

Swabs

patient's record

tweezers

adhesive tape

pills

The Checkup

The doctor's office is where you go for a checkup. The doctor wants to make sure that you are healthy. Next time that you are in the doctor's office, ask if you may listen to your own heartbeats with the stethoscope.

disposal pail

aunt

uncle

mother

father

parakeet

dog

photographer

camera

grandmother

grandfather

sister

puppies

The Family and Its Pets

This family and some of its pets are having a picture taken. Oh, my! Look what else is happening.

tripod

kittens

teddy bear

frog

mobile

cousins

baby carriage

cousin

playpen

goldfish

brother

hamster

stroller

baby

bib

turtle

diaper

bottle

rattle

bootees

41

The Countryside

The countryside is a great place for vacations, fishing, and having picnics. Farmers live and work there, too. Take a walk in the country. Walk softly and look carefully. You will see birds and many other animals, as well as flowers and trees.

trees

waterfall

forest

sailboat

lake

picnic table

campsite

bird

No Hunting

squirrel

bridge

WILDLIFE PRESERVE

stream

backpack

fishing pole

hiker

canteen

woodland trail

walking stick

flowers

hiking boots

mountain

farm

tollbooth

bridge

river

highway

MOTEL

roadside stand

parking lot

bushes

skunk

binoculars

tent

rowboat

campfire

birdwatcher

43

windmill

weather vane

apple orchard

field

beehives

farmhouse

billy goat

pump

rocking chair

nanny goat

kid

porch

vegetable garden

rake

mailbox

dog

hay bales

stone wall

pickup truck

The Farm

The farmer and his wife, the children, and the farmhands are all kept busy taking care of the crops and the animals on the farm. Even the cat may get up to chase away the mice—when he is not too busy sleeping.

geese

44

crows

scarecrow

silo

lightning rod

toolbox

pasture

farmhand

ducks

meadow

sheep

pond

hayloft

ladder

barn

safety glasses

horse

chain saw

plow

farmer

water trough

calf

cows

tractor

pail

hens

piglets

mud

chicks

pigs

pigpen

rooster

The Ranch

A ranch is a very large farm where cattle, horses, or sheep are raised. Sometimes helicopters help the cowboys at round-up time when the herds are brought in to be checked and branded.

cowboy

windmill

mesa

bunkhouse

bandanna

mane

horse

quirt

ten-gallon hat

vest

saddle

blanket

bridle

bit

reins

chaps

spur

stirrup

boots

cactus

hoof

helicopter

desert

jeep

O·CAT·CORRAL

barbed-wire fence

cattle herd

lasso

steer

calf

branding iron

jeans

fire

The Seashore

The ocean meets the land at the seashore. Lots of people spend their vacations at the beach, or on the shores of lakes and rivers. Can you see someone with a sea gull on his head?

sun

lighthouse

sea gulls

lifeguard

dune buggy

beach umbrella

fence

jetty

surfer

sand dunes

sun hat

surfboard

sunglasses

waves

cool drink

snorkel

bathing suit

transistor radio

cooler

picnic basket

mask

flip-flops

sand

beach chair

suntan lotion

beach ball

hot dog

swimming trunks

book

beach towel

pebbles

tote bag

seashells

flippers

starfish

beach grass

clams

48

Outer Space

The galaxy in which we earthlings and cat-lings live is full of wonderful things: planets, moons, and stars, comets and meteors, spacecraft and artificial satellites. Astronauts are the explorers of our galaxy. Perhaps you may shuttle off into space one day!

spacecraft

space capsule

Mercury

radio waves

Venus

spacecraft

LEM

Moon

Sun

footprints

astronaut

crater

Jupiter

Uranus

Neptune

Pluto

moons

Saturn

rings

star

asteroids

comet

spacecraft

Mars

fuel
tanks

space
shuttle

telescope

space
station

Earth

lift-off

dish antenna

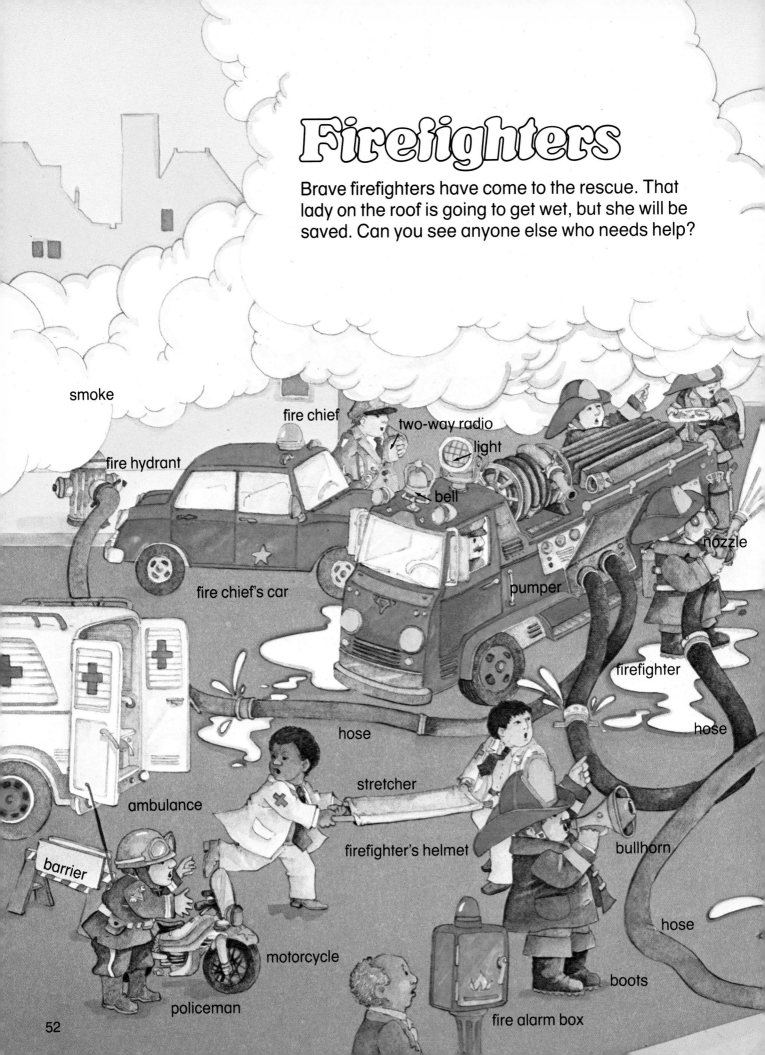

Firefighters

Brave firefighters have come to the rescue. That lady on the roof is going to get wet, but she will be saved. Can you see anyone else who needs help?

smoke

fire chief

two-way radio

light

fire hydrant

bell

nozzle

fire chief's car

pumper

firefighter

hose

hose

stretcher

ambulance

hose

firefighter's helmet

bullhorn

barrier

boots

motorcycle

policeman

fire alarm box

smoke

gas mask

oxygen tanks

firefighter

water

fire

rescue net

hose

ladder

ax

light

chimney

ax

firefighter

crossing guard

STOP

hook-and-ladder truck

firefighter

puddle

fire hydrant

53

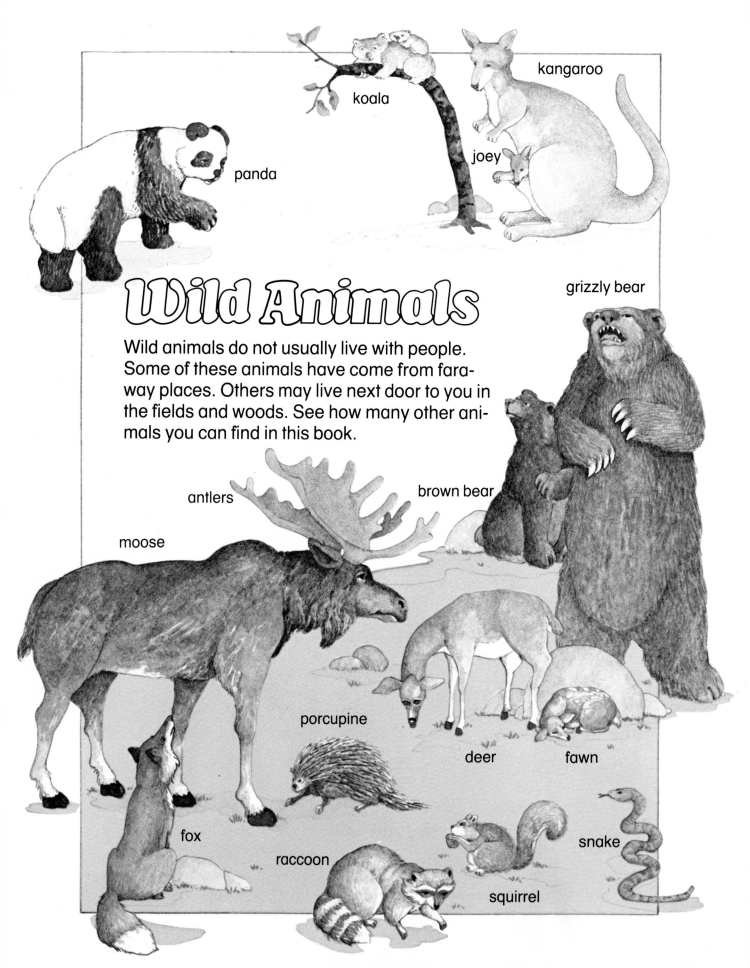

koala

kangaroo

joey

panda

grizzly bear

Wild Animals

Wild animals do not usually live with people. Some of these animals have come from faraway places. Others may live next door to you in the fields and woods. See how many other animals you can find in this book.

antlers

brown bear

moose

porcupine

deer

fawn

fox

snake

raccoon

squirrel

rhinoceros

tiger

giraffe

elephant

lion

zebra

frog

monkey

gorilla

alligator

hippopotamus

osprey

blue jay

robin

flock of geese

hawk

crow

oriole

owl

eagle

cardinals

tanager

starling

Canada goose

heron

pelican

flamingo

roadrunner

gosling

spoonbill

cattails

swan

cygnets

duck

Birds

Birds come in all sizes, from the tiny, jewel-like hummingbird to the mighty eagle. All birds have feathers and most of them fly. They live in woodlands and prairies, on mountains, in jungles and deserts, and even in cities. Baby birds hatch from eggs that the mother bird lays in a nest.

mourning dove

sparrow

woodpecker

goldfinch

meadowlark

pheasant

peacock

swift

hummingbird

parakeet

ibis

bird of paradise

parrot

toucan

cockroach

cricket

branch

Plants and Insects

Plants grow from seeds. Trees are the biggest plants of all. Honeybees and other insects carry pollen from one flower to another so that more plants may grow. All insects hatch from tiny eggs. Did you know that caterpillars turn into beautiful butterflies and moths?

dragonfly

housefly

mosquito

rose

poppy

petals

firefly

daisy

butterfly

ants

stem

leaves

thorn

dandelion

bud

violet

mushrooms

cactus

clover

grasshopper

moss

grass

58

honeybee

wasp

caterpillar

tree
trunk

butterfly

bumblebee

beetle

moth

buttercup

ladybug

praying
mantis

black-eyed
Susan

fern

walking
stick

spider web

branch

ivy

wooly bear

roots

spider

Sea Animals

There are thousands of fish and other animals in the ocean. Did you know that the blue whale is the biggest animal that has ever lived? Whales and dolphins are not fish. They have to come up for air. Scuba divers carry air tanks on their backs. Can you see a scuba diver?

flying fish

fins

gills

manta ray

shark

tentacles

octopus

school of sardines

eel

suckers

jellyfish

sea horses

dolphin

baby dolphin

coral

swordfish

seal

walrus

penguins

ice floe

baby seal

tunas

sea furtle

flippers

whale

61

brontosaurus

tyrannosaurus

trachodon

ornitholestes

stegosaurus

visitors

spiky tail

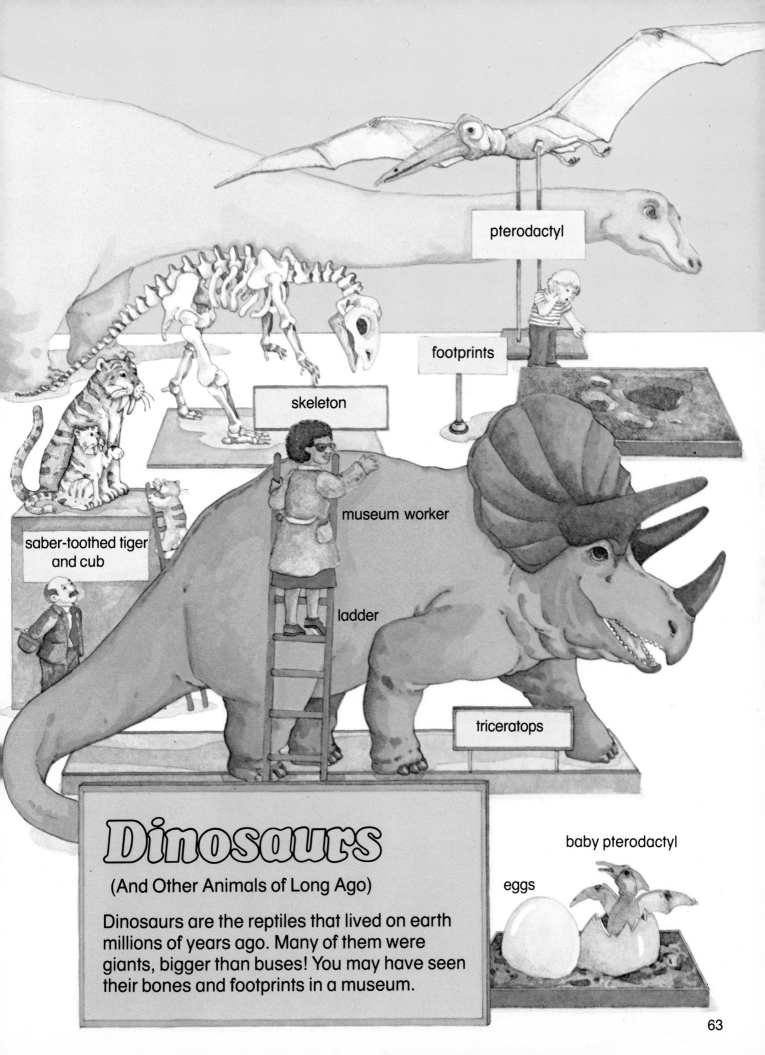

pterodactyl

footprints

skeleton

museum worker

saber-toothed tiger
and cub

ladder

triceratops

baby pterodactyl

eggs

Dinosaurs

(And Other Animals of Long Ago)

Dinosaurs are the reptiles that lived on earth millions of years ago. Many of them were giants, bigger than buses! You may have seen their bones and footprints in a museum.

Keeping in Touch

There are many ways to "keep in touch." You can write a letter, send a postcard, and call by telephone. Television, movies, and radio also keep us in touch. Don't forget newspapers, magazines, and books.

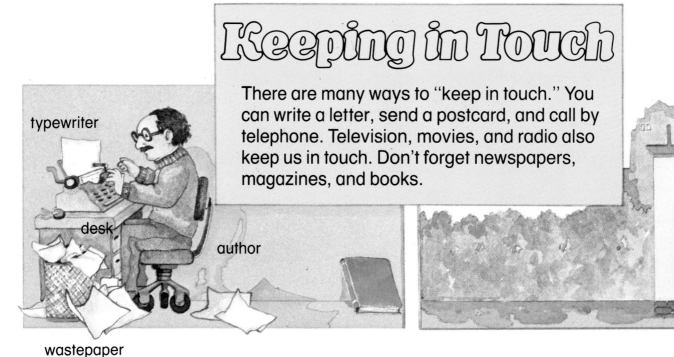

typewriter

desk

author

wastepaper basket

telephone

OPERATORS

telephone switchboard

writer

envelope

stamp

postcard

mail carrier

mail cart

BOOKSTORE

books

newspapers

magazines

reader

Hello! I feel better.

ring!

mailbox

letter

Control Booth

television studio

light

microphone

boom

camera crew

camera

actor

television set

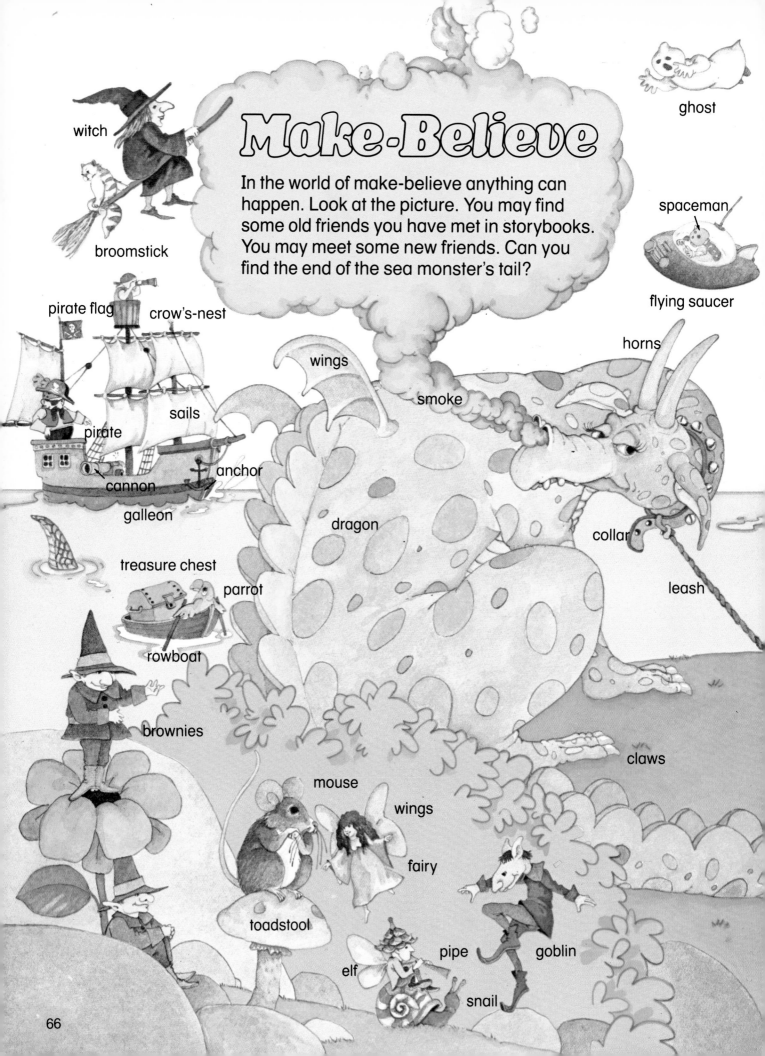

witch

broomstick

ghost

spaceman

flying saucer

Make-Believe

In the world of make-believe anything can happen. Look at the picture. You may find some old friends you have met in storybooks. You may meet some new friends. Can you find the end of the sea monster's tail?

pirate flag

crow's-nest

wings

smoke

horns

sails

pirate

cannon

anchor

collar

galleon

dragon

leash

treasure chest

parrot

rowboat

brownies

claws

mouse

wings

fairy

toadstool

elf

pipe

goblin

snail

66

superhero

supergirl

superpicnic

cloud

supercat

sultan

flying carpet

giant

flag

crown

turret

king

queen

island

window box

sea monster

sword

enchanted forest

castle

magic stars

chains

knight in armor

horse in armor

cap

drawbridge

little monster

fairy godmother

dungeon

book of spells

wizard

troll

magic wand

frog prince

spiky tail

monster

moat

67

Counting

At last all the cats in the book have come out of hiding. Each one is wearing a number on its T-shirt. Can you count the cats from one to ten?

Telling Time

When the sun comes up, it's morning. It's time to get up! Clocks and watches tell us what time it is. Which time do you like best: getting-up time, lunch time, or going-to-bed time? Cats like catnap time.

minute hand

hour hand

clock

GOING-TO-SCHOOL TIME

tower clock

SCHOOL

GETTING-UP TIME

alarm clock

LUNCH TIME

electric clock

wristwatch

BATHTIME

grandfather clock

digital clock

BEDTIME

STORY TIME

diamond

crescent

circle

cone

oval

sphere

rectangle

pyramid

star

cube

triangle

Shapes

Everything around you has some kind of a shape. Is your window a square or a rectangle? Can you see a crescent moon, or a round moon? Be sure to wish upon a ☆ !

square

heart

purple

orange

green

red

paintbrush

brown

white

blue

yellow

Colors

Colors are all around you. When you mix paints together you can make new colors. What happens if you mix blue and yellow? What is your favorite color?

black

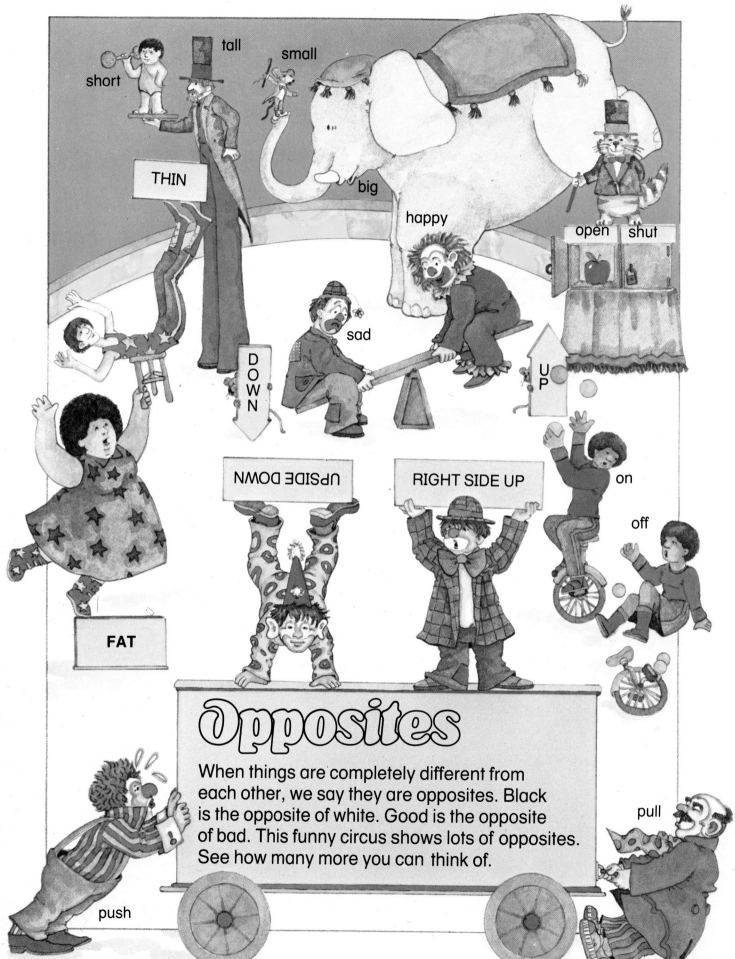

short

tall

small

THIN

big

happy

open shut

sad

DOWN

UP

UPSIDE DOWN

RIGHT SIDE UP

on

off

FAT

Opposites

When things are completely different from each other, we say they are opposites. Black is the opposite of white. Good is the opposite of bad. This funny circus shows lots of opposites. See how many more you can think of.

pull

push

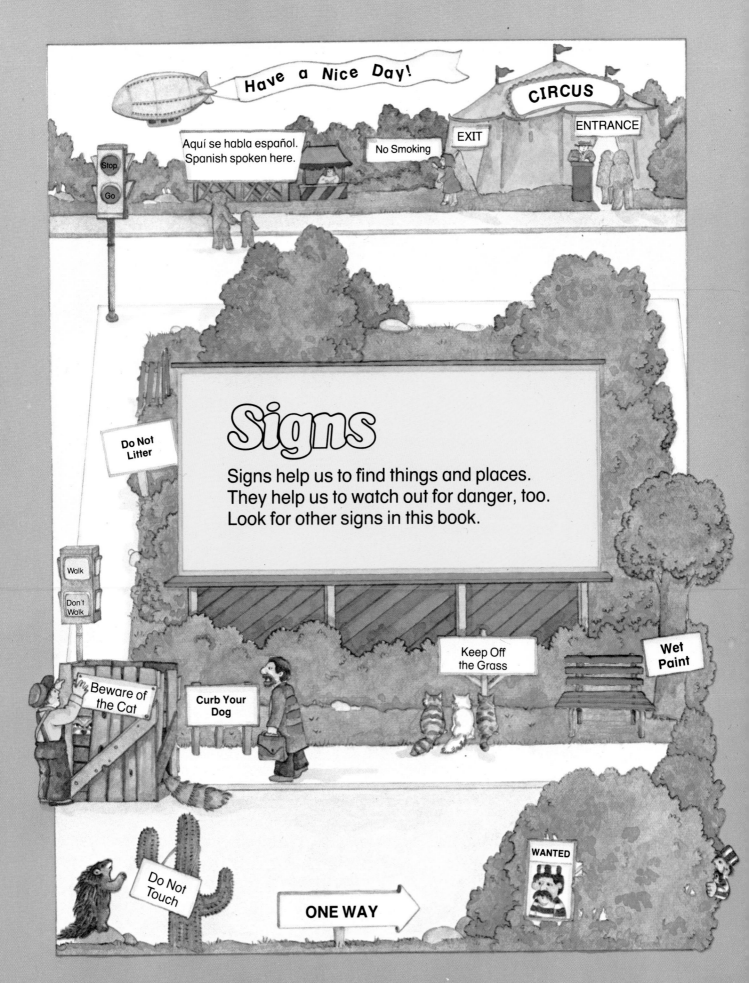

Signs

Signs help us to find things and places.
They help us to watch out for danger, too.
Look for other signs in this book.

Tools

file

Tools are objects that people have made to help them in their work or in their hobbies. Here are tools to use in the house and tools to use outdoors. See how many tools you can find on other pages.

pliers

plane

screwdriver

bolt

screws

nuts

nails

hammer

sandpaper

folding ruler

chisel

drill

wrench

coping saw

harp

recorder

harmonica

clarinet

accordion

trumpet

bagpipe

violin

French horn

bugle

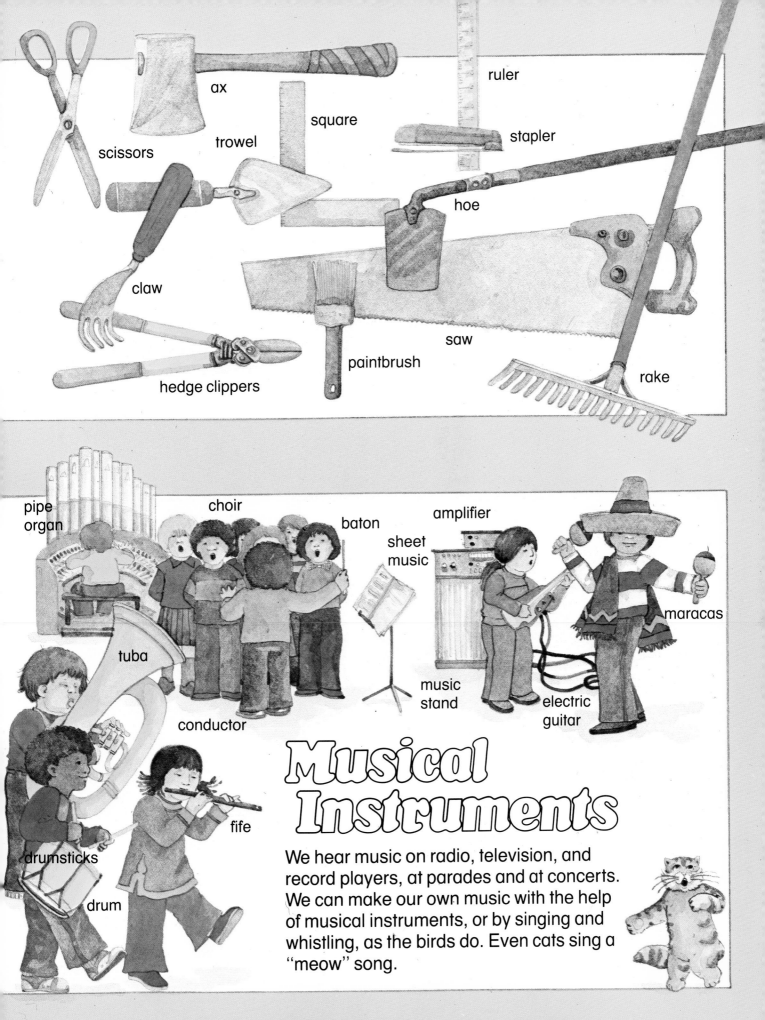

scissors

ax

trowel

square

ruler

stapler

hoe

claw

hedge clippers

paintbrush

saw

rake

pipe organ

choir

baton

amplifier

sheet music

maracas

tuba

music stand

electric guitar

conductor

drumsticks

fife

drum

Musical Instruments

We hear music on radio, television, and record players, at parades and at concerts. We can make our own music with the help of musical instruments, or by singing and whistling, as the birds do. Even cats sing a "meow" song.

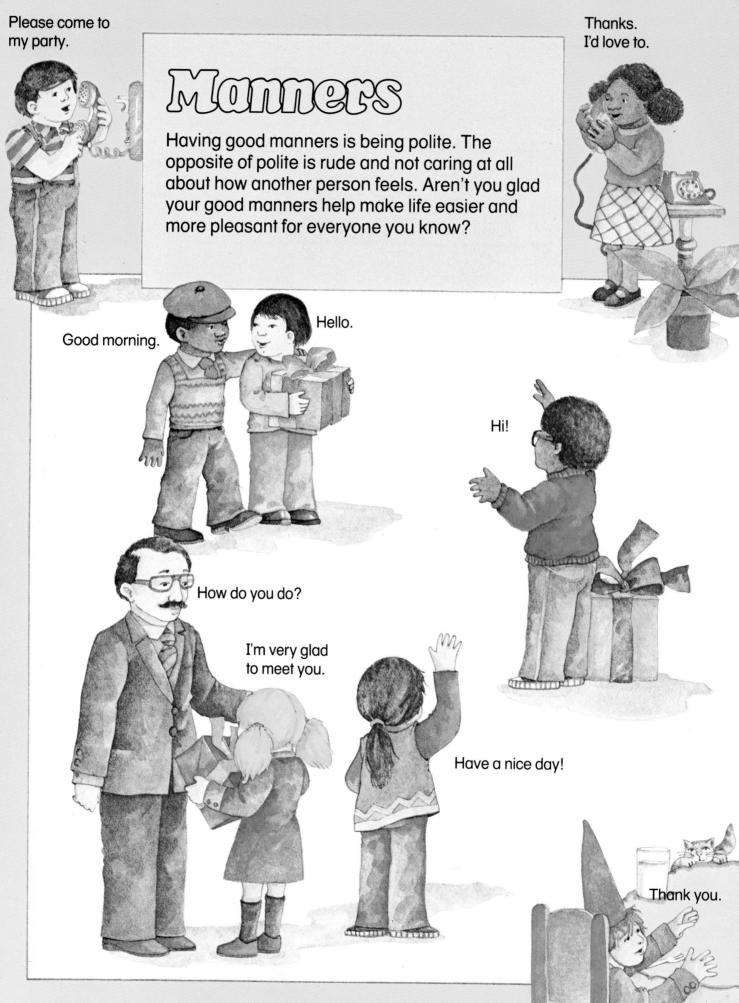

Please come to my party.

Thanks. I'd love to.

Manners

Having good manners is being polite. The opposite of polite is rude and not caring at all about how another person feels. Aren't you glad your good manners help make life easier and more pleasant for everyone you know?

Good morning.

Hello.

Hi!

How do you do?

I'm very glad to meet you.

Have a nice day!

Thank you.

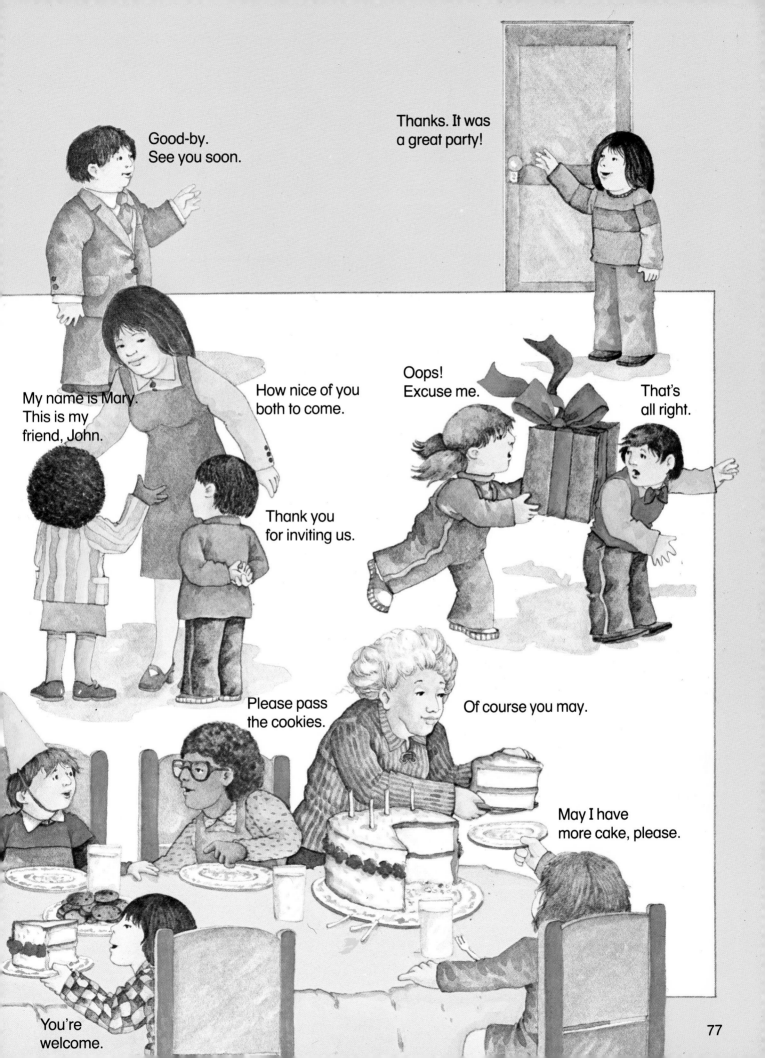

Apple-Pie ABC

Here is a story about an apple pie and the 26 letters of the alphabet. Try making up your own story, using each letter from A to Z.

A was an apple pie.

Elephant eyed it.

Fox fled with it.

Gorilla grabbed it back.

Koala kissed it.

Lion looked after it.

Monkey marched to the table with it.

Quail quartered it.

Rhinoceros roared for it.

Snake sat down for a bite.

Walrus wept for it.

Xenops x-rayed it.

Yak yelled yum-yum for it.

Bb

Bear baked it.

Cc

Cat clawed it.

Dd

Dog dreamed about it.

Hh

Hippopotamus held onto it.

Ii

Inchworm inched around it.

Jj

Jaguar jumped for it.

Nn

Nanny goat nibbled at it.

Oo

Ostrich observed it.

Pp

Pig peeped at it.

Tt

Tiger tasted it, too.

Uu

Unicorn upset it.

Vv

Vole viewed it.

Zz

Zebra zoomed in and ate the rest of it.

The End

And that was the end of the apple pie.

Good Night!

Night is the time when most people and animals sleep. But some people, such as bakers and night watchmen, are at work. And some animals leave their babies in their cozy homes and go out hunting for food.

fox

garbage can

tree hollow

raccoons

birds

nest

rabbits

doghouse

kittens

basket

cat

dog

puppies

lamp

good night

child

bed

slippers